# THE CARE AND CONSERVATION OF GRAVEYARDS

**OPW**

*Oifig na nOibreacha Poiblí*
*The Office of Public Works*

ISBN 07076 1614 X

© Government of Ireland, 1995

**Text and research**
Edward Bourke, Margaret Keane, Sean Kirwan (National Monuments and Historic Properties Service, OPW), Tom Curtis and Eamon Grennan (National Parks and Wildlife Service, OPW).

**Editing**
Elizabeth FitzPatrick

**Illustrations and cover design**
Karen Cronin

**Photography**
John Scarry (OPW)

**Design, typesetting and layout**
Wordwell Ltd

**Colour separations**
**Grants and Wordwell Ltd**

### Dublin
Published by the Stationery Office
To be purchased through any bookseller, or directly from the Government Publications Sales Office, Sun Alliance House, Molesworth St, Dublin 2

# CONTENTS

| | |
|---|---|
| Introduction | 5 |
| The role of the Office of Public Works | 6 |
| Ownership and the law | 7 |
| Funding graveyard schemes and conditions of approval | 8 |
| Planning for care and maintenance | 9 |
| The importance of expert advice | 10 |
| Clearing vegetation | 11 |
| Dealing with ground surface | 13 |
| Surveying the site | 14 |
| Deciding on the scope of further work | 15 |
| Care of gravestones | 16 |
| Conservation of boundary walls and buildings | 17 |
| Graveyard extensions | 18 |
| What to do and what not to do | 19 |
| Recommended reading | 22 |
| Useful addresses | 23 |

Graveyards are an important part of our archaeological heritage and should accordingly be treated with respect.

## INTRODUCTION

Graveyards are an important feature of the historic landscape and frequently provide clues to understanding our past. In recent years the increased awareness among local communities of the importance of these sites has inspired many graveyard clean-up schemes. While well-founded projects can enhance the appearance of old graveyards and simultaneously fulfill an important educational role, ill-conceived graveyard schemes can do untold damage.

The purpose of this booklet is to offer advice to those caring for or cleaning up graveyards and to encourage careful planning of any such developments. The best possible advice should be sought from the outset and adhered to throughout a scheme.

Finely crafted decorative ironwork often surrounds box-tombs, table-tombs and family plots.

## THE ROLE OF THE OFFICE OF PUBLIC WORKS (OPW)

The protection, maintenance and presentation of national monuments and historic sites in State care, including some graveyards, has been a very important aspect of the work of the OPW since the 1870s. It has a legal role to play in the protection of old graveyards, under the National Monuments Acts 1930–94. Consequently, this booklet is designed to provide general guidelines on how to make the best of an old graveyard and at the same time preserve and conserve its irreplaceable archaeological and historical heritage.

*Below* Old pathways and mature trees enhance the appearance of graveyards and should therefore be retained.

Medieval graveslab

## OWNERSHIP AND THE LAW

Before work is undertaken in a graveyard or a church within it, ownership and legal status should be checked carefully. Old graveyards and churches are generally owned by a local authority, the Church of Ireland, or the OPW. In some cases a graveyard may be the property of a private individual and as with any other property, the owner's permission is required before any work can be carried out there.

It should be noted that under the 1930 National Monuments Act, as amended in 1987, it is an offence to carry out works on any national monument (a term which includes old graveyards and structures within them) in the ownership or guardianship of a local authority without the consent in writing of both the Commissioners of Public Works and the authority concerned. Under the 1994 National Monuments Amendment Act, anyone wishing to carry out work on a site or monument listed in the OPW Sites and Monuments Record is obliged to notify that office and may not initiate work within two months of the date of notification, without OPW approval. Failure to comply with the legal requirements may result in prosecution and severe penalties on conviction. No digging can be done on any archaeologically sensitive site except by a qualified archaeologist excavating under licence to the OPW. Unlicensed excavation is an offence under the National Monuments Acts and is severely punishable by law, as is the unlicensed use of a metal detector for the purpose of searching for archaeological artefacts.

Objects may be found during graveyard clean-up schemes. Common graveyard finds include ancient graveslabs, bullaun stones, quernstones, plain and sculpted architectural fragments. Any such finds must be reported to the Director, National Monuments and Historic Properties Service, OPW. There is also a legal requirement to report same to the Director of the National Museum, Kildare Street, Dublin 2, within four days.

## FUNDING GRAVEYARD SCHEMES AND CONDITIONS OF APPROVAL

Before starting a graveyard project it is important to consider how it will be funded. Clearly the amount needed will depend on the type of work envisaged. In a case where a graveyard is owned by a local authority, the possibility of funding for maintenance work from that authority should be clarified. In some instances funds may be available from FÁS for a graveyard clean-up. Should a local graveyard committee not have the necessary funds required to employ an archaeologist, it is advisable not to proceed with any works.

There are a number of conditions which must be met before a local graveyard scheme can receive approval. The OPW requires both a pre-conservation and post-conservation archaeological report on the site, prepared by a qualified archaeologist. The pre-conservation report should provide full details of the present condition of the graveyard and the archaeologist's advice and recommendations as to the nature of the works required. The post-conservation report should include a comprehensive survey of the site, describe in full all the works carried out and incorporate an inventory of any features and objects recovered. A letter of consent from the owner of the graveyard is also required.

In the case of a potential FÁS-funded scheme, an application for funding will not be entertained without an accompanying archaeological report. An additional FÁS approval form, which may be obtained from your local FÁS office, should be completed by the archaeologist, and accompany the main report.

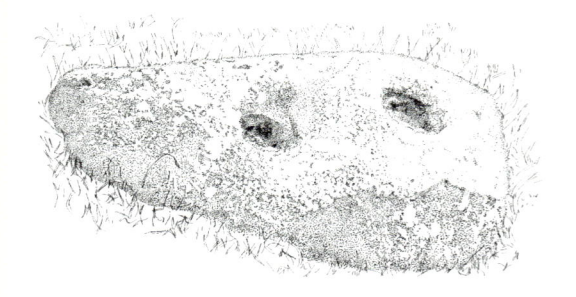

Bullaun stone

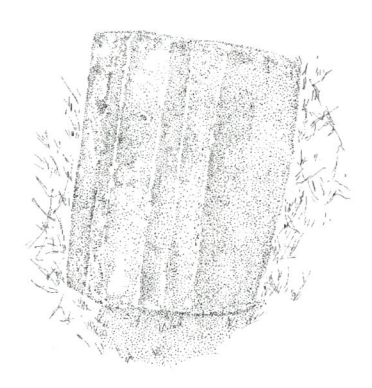

Jambstone from a doorway

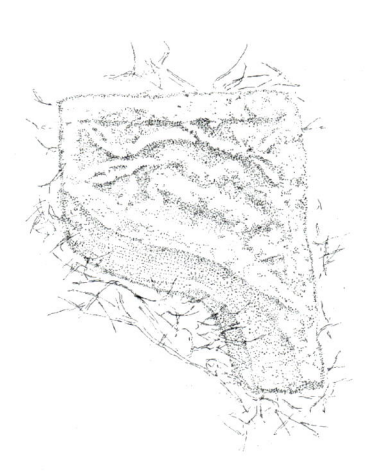

*Decorative window fragment*

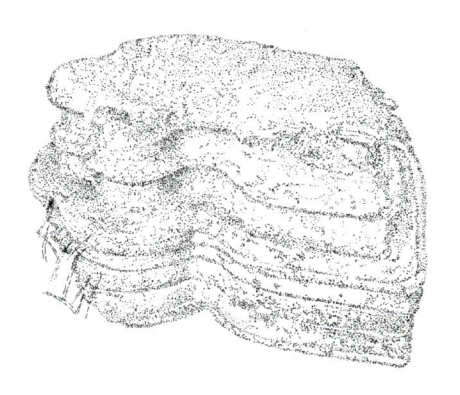

*Moulded column base*

## PLANNING FOR CARE AND MAINTENANCE

The first thing involved in caring for a graveyard is to decide, in consultation with an archaeologist, how much work you wish to do, how much you or your community can afford to spend, and how much alteration to a site is desirable. As a general rule, you should endeavour to alter the site as little as possible, indeed in the majority of cases, it is recommended that graveyard schemes limit themselves to vegetation clearance in an ecologically sensitive way. Judicious clearance of rank growth, striking a balance between the ecology and archaeology of the site, can leave a graveyard looking most attractive.

Graveyards are an integral part of local heritage and frequently contain the sites or standing remains of early churches and archaeological monuments and are generally home to a diversity of plant and animal life. Bearing this in mind, great care should be taken in planning each stage of a clean-up project.

As the clearance of vegetation will affect both the archaeology of the site and its wildlife, you should consult the local OPW wildlife ranger, in addition to the archaeologist, for practical advice at planning stage. The 1976 Wildlife Act states that it is an offence to destroy, by any means, growing vegetation on uncultivated land between 15th April and 31st August in any year. In the light of this, it would be best to plan your scheme accordingly, more particularly in the case of a heavily overgrown graveyard which has become a habitat for wild plants, birds and hedgerow animals. It should also be noted that there is a suite of 68 flowering plants protected under the Flora Protection Order and it requires a licence to interfere with their habitat. Some species on this list occasionally occur in graveyards, for example *Lanceolate Spleenwort,* a fern which grows on walls.

## THE IMPORTANCE OF EXPERT ADVICE

In some cases the work envisaged will require practical skills and expertise which may not be available locally. Therefore, in planning your budget, allowances should be made for employing surveyors, masons etc. Taking on more than you can manage, with the result that the graveyard is left in a worse state than it was originally, is to be avoided. In this regard, seeking the prior advice of experts will ensure a realistic projection of what can be achieved with available financial and human resources. The experts will help you to prepare a phased plan, each stage of which can be completed independently, bringing with it a significant improvement to the graveyard.

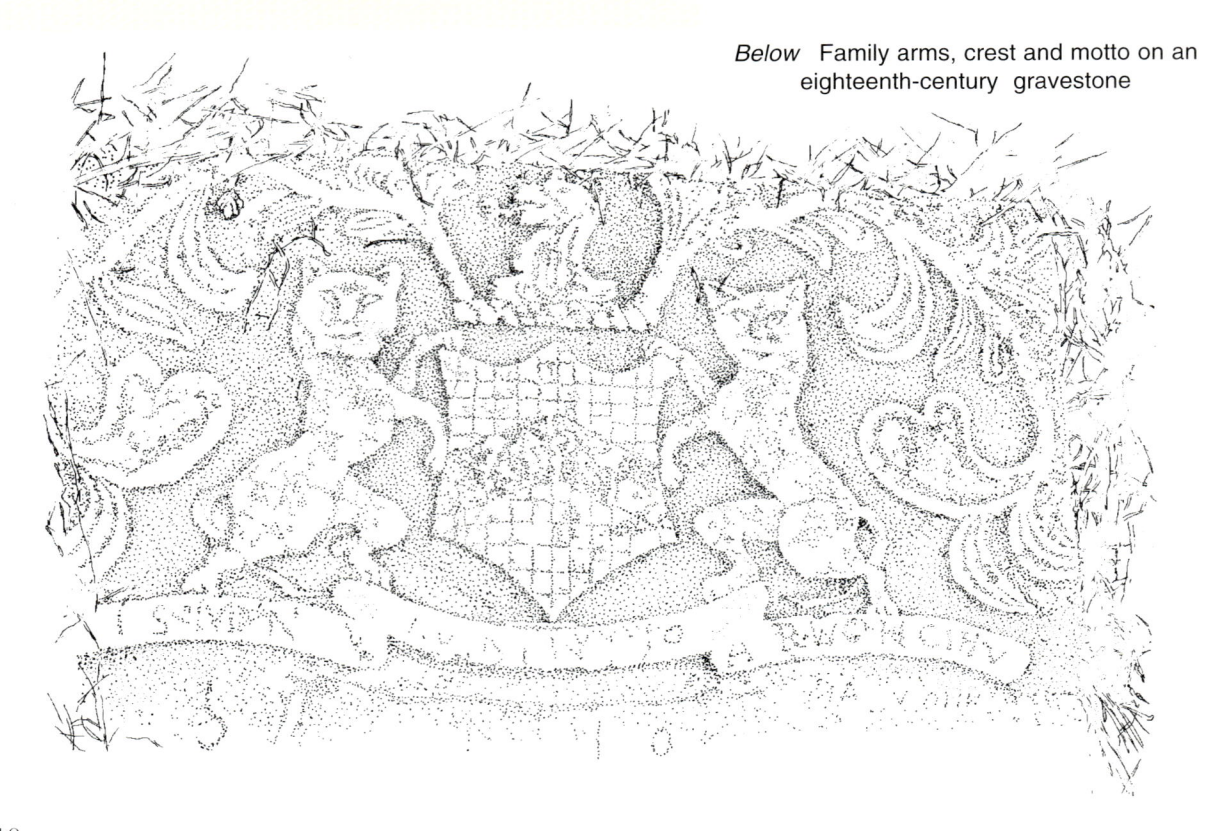

*Below* Family arms, crest and motto on an eighteenth-century gravestone

Early cross-head with inscription

Early cross-inscribed stone

## CLEARING VEGETATION

Many graveyards are heavily overgrown. The clearance of that vegetation will affect both the archaeology and wildlife of the site. The dense undergrowth of bushes, briars, weeds and fallen branches may conceal ruined buildings and a variety of graveyard artefacts, among them ancient and relatively modern grave-markers, old vaults, baptismal fonts and stoups, stone mortars, quernstones, bullaun stones, cross fragments and decorative wrought-iron railings.

Old graveyards are also good habitats for a variety of insects, birds and mammals. Ivy-covered walls and ruins may be the home of bats and barn owls, while tall trees provide nesting sites for kestrels, sparrow-hawks, rooks and jackdaws. Boundary hedges and scrub support a variety of birds such as thrushes, blackbirds, robins, wrens, tits and finches. In heavily farmed land, graveyards may be the only oasis left for some varieties of wildlife including grassland flora. Therefore, the removal of vegetation should be done in a judicious way so that, where possible, some is left for the benefit of the wildlife. The advice of a botanist is recommended for this important phase in a graveyard clean-up.

There are a number of very important general rules to be observed when clearing vegetation. Undergrowth should only be cleared by hand, using scythes, slash-hooks or strimmers. The burning of vegetation on site seriously damages buildings and gravestones and should be avoided at all costs. Likewise, the use of broad-spectrum weedkiller is not recommended. In instances where it has been used, a noticeable decline in wild plants and wildlife has followed, and in time, a prolific rejuvenation of weeds has ensued, defeating the original purpose. In particular, ivy should never be removed from buildings without professional advice. Pulling off ivy can destabilize a structure, endangering graveyard visitors, and can often hasten its total collapse. The removal of ivy from trees is also not recommended as, contrary to popular opinion it does not damage trees but provides a valuable ecological habitat for birds and insects. Never uproot plants and trees. If they are rotten or dangerous they should be cut close to ground level and treated in order to accelerate the rotting process. Once the site is cleared it is important to plan for its regular maintenance, otherwise all your hard work and commitment will have been wasted.

*Above* The Lesser Celandine *(Ranunculus ficaria)*, a native wild flower, thrives in the graveyard environment.

## DEALING WITH GROUND SURFACE

Under no circumstances should a graveyard ever be levelled off. The hummocks and hollows so characteristic of old graveyards frequently cover archaeological features such as wall-footings of early buildings, burials or ancient ditches. A mechanical digger should never be used in a graveyard.

All earthfast stones and gravestones should be left in the ground. Collapsed masonry from an ancient building within a graveyard may only be cleared under archaeological supervision. Any loose cut-stone architectural fragments found scattered about should be collected and carefully put aside in an area of the graveyard designated specifically for that purpose. The OPW and the National Museum should be contacted and informed about these objects. Earthfast cut stones should be left in position as they may well mark the sites of later graves.

*Below* Humps and hollows in ground surface are often indicative of underlying archaeological features.

## SURVEYING THE SITE

Once the site has been cleared, it is important to record carefully the location of all gravestones and their inscriptions, sculptural fragments, old walls, and other features, in consultation with your archaeologist. A full record of the graveyard prior to any alteration is essential in interpreting the site accurately.

The results of your survey can produce useful information on the archaeology and local history of the site, some of which you may choose to display on a sign at the entrance to the graveyard, for the benefit of visitors. Alternatively you may wish to publish your discoveries as a booklet, including a record of all gravestone inscriptions.

The bibliography which accompanies this booklet includes two works which explain how to record ancient graveyards.

*Below* Panel of a seventeenth-century altar-tomb, decorated with instruments of the Passion

## DECIDING ON THE SCOPE OF FURTHER WORK

While the majority of graveyard schemes are considered complete following vegetation clearance and necessary repairs to boundary walls, in certain cases a project may be deemed suitable for conservation work to gravestones and buildings. It must be stressed that archaeological and architectural expertise, as well as skillful artisans with a knowledge of medieval masonry, are a prerequisite for any conservation work on an ancient building.

On the ecological side, you may decide to plant areas of the graveyard with trees and flowering plants. If circumstances allow for the planting of trees, native species such as oak, ash and wild cherry should be chosen. The planting of wild flowers is not recommended unless done under the guidance of an expert botanist.

*Below* Headstones lying at odd angles are part of the charm of an old graveyard.

## CARE OF GRAVESTONES

Unless graveslabs and headstones are in danger of falling or breaking, it is almost always best to leave them as they are. Straightening graveslabs involves disturbing the ground, thereby interfering with burials. Box-tombs and table-tombs should not be moved or reconstructed without professional advice. Often these tombs and gravestones lend the graveyard its character and any attempt to lay the site out like a modern graveyard should be avoided.

If it is decided that there are good reasons for straightening selected gravestones, or that it is necessary to repair broken ones and conserve railings around monuments, this should only be carried out if the supervising archaeologist is satisfied that the appropriate expertise is available to do so, otherwise much damage may be done to the site.

In general, cleaning of gravestones should only be carried out after careful consideration, because of the risk of damage to the inscriptions and escalating the rate of erosion of the stone. Sandblasting should not even be considered. If cleaning is done, it should only be with soft brushes and water. Abrasive materials or brushes and strong cleaning agents should never be used. It should be remembered for instance, that lichens growing on gravestones can be interesting features. Lichens have a role to play in allowing us to monitor pollution and in some cases they may also help us to estimate the age of a stone feature. A record of each gravestone inscription can be taken by making a rubbing or squeeze. In this way you can achieve a permanent record of all inscriptions without damaging them.

Eighteenth-century headstones

*Above* The use of cement mortar and ribbon pointing, as shown here, is inappropriate in the conservation of medieval buildings.

## CONSERVATION OF BOUNDARY WALLS AND BUILDINGS

Many graveyards are enclosed by attractive stone walls which occasionally incorporate ancient architectural fragments in their fabric and support interesting plant life. If a boundary wall is in need of repair, expert advice should be sought before any work commences. In general it is advocated that only very necessary repairs be undertaken. Existing masonry coursing should be maintained and correct mortars with flush or recessed pointing used at all times. It should be noted that ribbon pointing is inappropriate for an old wall. Under no circumstances should an existing boundary wall be pulled down.

You are strongly advised not to remove ivy from a building as invariably this will cause the total collapse of the structure concerned. Cutting ivy at the roots and letting it die back, may leave a building in need of immediate conservation. In this instance, the advice of an architect or archaeologist is absolutely necessary before cutting ivy and during all subsequent conservation work. An architectural survey is an essential first step in any building conservation programme. On the practical side, skilled masons must be employed, scaffolding may need to be erected and correct mortars chosen. In cases where skilled artisans are unavailable, or too expensive, it may be necessary to fence off an area of the graveyard for safety reasons and leave the structure alone.

If it is decided that a certain amount of repointing of walls and buildings is appropriate for the site, expert advice is again required. Prior to such work being approved, a full survey of the structures to be conserved must be carried out by an architect or surveyor with experience of early buildings. Seeking such advice will prevent damage to structural remains and ensure a high quality of conservation work.

## GRAVEYARD EXTENSIONS

The archaeological implications of extending an old graveyard should be assessed before any step is taken to acquire land or draw up plans. In the case of many old graveyards, the area outside the graveyard wall can be even more important archaeologically than the area within. Consequently it is often advisable to open a completely new graveyard at least 100 metres away from the old one.

New plots should not be laid out in old graveyards because they will usually disturb archaeological deposits or previous burials that are not marked.

*Below* Old graveyard boundary walls are a choice habitat for the common fern, Maidenhair Spleenwort (*Asplenium trichomanes*).

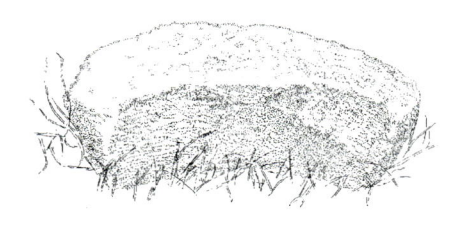

Arch-stone

Medieval keystone decorated with a bishop's head

## DO

✓ Check the ownership and legal status of the graveyard and the structures within it, and seek the owner's permission to do work there.

✓ Contact both the National Monuments and Historic Properties Service, and the Wildlife Service, OPW before you commence your scheme.

✓ Plan out the programme of work carefully, beginning with the least difficult tasks.

✓ Clear the site using only hand strimmers or other hand tools.

✓ Designate dump sites away from monuments.

✓ Survey the site, marking in the church, any other buildings and all gravestones and memorials.

✓ Retain healthy trees, and if planting new trees, choose native species.

✓ Leave all hummocks in the ground, they may mark structural and archaeological features.

✓ Maintain existing pathways using gravel, small stones and grit.

✓ Keep boundary walls, banks and hedges.

✓ Wait until the site is cleared to decide on conservation of structural remains.

✓ Keep all architectural and sculptural fragments, record their position and report their finding to the OPW and the National Museum.

## DO NOT

✗ Do not start without professional advice and a plan to work to.

✗ Do not try to demolish or remove anything from the site without the landowner's permission and the approval of the Office of Public Works.

✗ Do not dig graves near walls, they can cause structural damage.

✗ Do not attempt unlicensed excavation, it is illegal (this includes removal of rubble from collapsed walls).

✗ Do not use machinery to clear or level the site.

✗ Do not burn off vegetation, or use total spectrum weedkillers.

✗ Do not plant wild plants without expert consultation.

✗ Do not uproot ivy, trees, plants or gravestones.

✗ Do not pull ivy off buildings or trees.

✗ Do not pull ivy off fragile gravestones or composite tombs/memorials.

✗ Do not use wire brushes or sandblasters.

✗ Do not apply paint to gravestone inscriptions.

✗ Do not repoint any masonry without professional advice.

✗ Do not use ribbon pointing on old boundary walls or buildings.

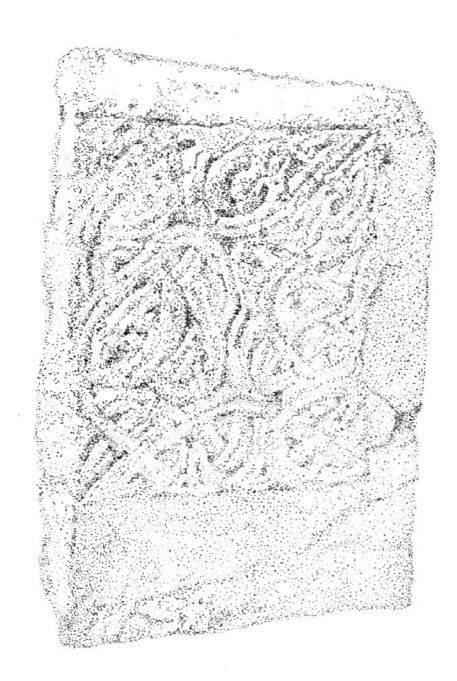

Early cut-stone fragment decorated with elaborate interlace

✗ Do not level off pathways.

✗ Do not use graveslabs for paving.

✗ Do not lay new pathways without consulting an archaeologist.

✗ Do not move gravestones unnecessarily or without archaeological advice and supervision.

✗ Do not burn rubbish on site, close to buildings or gravestones.

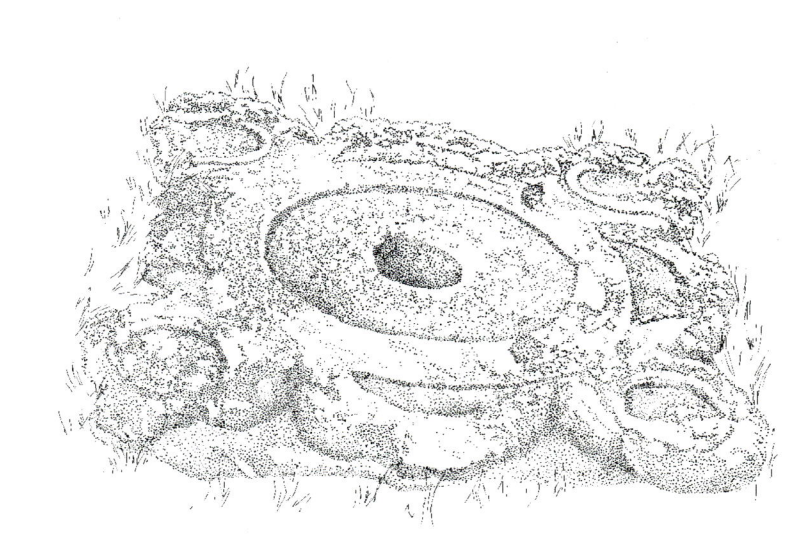

Medieval table-font base

# RECOMMENDED READING

Anon, *Report of the commissioners of church temporalities in Ireland in the period 1869–80* (Dublin, 1881), 107–34.

T.G.F. Curtis and H.N. McGough, *The Irish Red Data Book: vascular plants* (Dublin, 1988).

K. de hÓra, 'Church and graveyard cleaning and conservation' in *Journal of the Galway Archaeological and Historical Society*, vol. 41 (1987–8), 126–31.

A. Hamlin, *The care of graveyards* (Department of the Environment for Northern Ireland, 1983).

J. Jones, *How to record graveyards* (Council for British Archaeology and Rescue, London, 1984).

H.G. Leask, *Irish churches and monastic buildings*, 3 vols (Dundalk, 1955–60).

P. McCullough, U. McDermot and M. McMahon, *Recording the past from ancient churchyards and other sources* (Dublin Archaeological Society, 1987).

M.J.P. Scannell and D.M. Synnott, *Census catalogue of the flora of Ireland* (Dublin, 1987).

D.A. Webb, *An Irish flora* (Dundalk, 1977).

**USEFUL ADDRESSES**

The Director,
National Monuments and Historic Properties Service,
Office of Public Works,
51 St Stephen's Green,
Dublin 2.

The Director,
The National Parks and Wildlife Service,
Office of Public Works,
51 St Stephen's Green,
Dublin 2.
Telephone (01) 6613111
Fax (01) 6610747

The Director,
National Museum of Ireland,
Kildare St.,
Dublin 2.
Telephone (01) 6618811
Fax (01) 6766116

FÁS —The Training Authority,
Head Office,
27 Upper Baggot Street,
Dublin 4.
Telephone (01) 6685777
Fax (01) 6682691